MARTIAL ARTS

KICK-BOXING

www.raintreepublishers.co.uk

To order:
Phone 44 (0) 1865 888112
Send a fax to 44 (0) 1865 314091
Visit the Raintree bookshop at
www.raintreepublishers.co.uk
to browse our catalogue and order online.

Produced by
David West Children's Books
7 Princeton Court
55 Felsham Road
London SW15 1AZ

Photographer: Sylvio Dokov
Designer: Gary Jeffrey
Editor: James Pickering

First published in Great Britain by
Raintree, Halley Court, Jordan Hill,
Oxford OX2 8EJ, part of Harcourt Education.
Raintree is a registered trademark of Harcourt
Education Ltd.

© David West Children's Books 2003
The moral right of the proprietor has been asserted.

Printed and bound in Italy

ISBN 1 844 21693 4 (hardback)
07 06 05 04 03
10 9 8 7 6 5 4 3 2 1

ISBN 1 844 21698 5 (paperback)
08 07 06 05 04
10 9 8 7 6 5 4 3 2 1

British Library Cataloguing in Publication Data
Nonnemacher, Klaus
Kick-boxing. – (Martial Arts)
796.8'3
A full catalogue record for this book is available
from the British Library.

Acknowledgements
The publishers would like to thank the following for
permission to reproduce photographs:

Abbreviations: t-top, m-middle, b-bottom, r-right,
l-left, c-centre.

Pages 6b, 11tl, 13br, 15b, 18tl, 25b (John Gichigi/
Allsport), 22tl (Paula Bronstein/ Liaison), 6t - Getty
Images. 21tr (GES), 24b (Michael Deubner) - Klaus
Nonnemacher.

Every effort has been made to contact copyright
holders of any material reproduced in this book.
Any omissions will be rectified in subsequent
printings if notice is given to the publishers.

Sylvio Dokov was born in Sofia, Bulgaria. For the
past two decades, he has been one of Europe's
leading martial arts photographers. Sylvio works
from his own studio in Telford, Shropshire.

THE AUTHOR
Klaus Nonnemacher is a
seven-times World
Champion in kick-boxing,
and currently the vice
president of the WKA.

THE MODELS
Left to right – Christopher
Pritchard, green belt,
Suzanne Grayson, orange
belt, Patrick Quinn, black
belt gold bar.

*An explanation of kick-boxing terms can be
found on page 31.*

MARTIAL ARTS

KICK-BOXING

Klaus Nonnemacher

Raintree

Contents

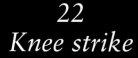

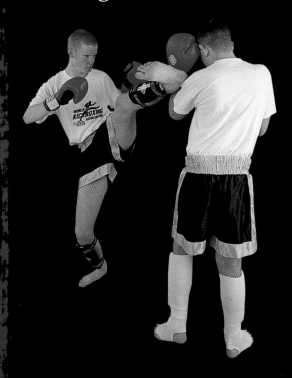

Introduction

Kick-boxing is a fast-growing sport that was established in the early 1970s. Today, it is practised all over the world. It reduces fat more effectively than almost any other sport, and develops muscles, stamina, co-ordination and fast reactions. It is also a strict mental discipline, involving clear rules. Concentration, combined with hard training, build up both your self-confidence and your level of fitness.

History

Joe Lewis in about 1963

Traditional martial arts from the Far East became popular in the USA after World War II (1939–45), especially karate. At first, competitors in karate tournaments were not allowed to make full contact with each other, because it was too dangerous. But competitors and fans alike became frustrated with these restrictions, and safety equipment was developed for full-contact karate. This sport evolved into modern kick-boxing when competitors adopted training techniques from boxing to improve their fitness. The American Joe Lewis became the first official World Heavyweight kick-boxing champion in 1974.

In its early years, the sport was known as full-contact karate.

Competitors in full-contact karate wore long trousers. The techniques in these early fights owed more to karate than to boxing.

Kit

Proper safety equipment is vital in modern kick-boxing, so that you can train safely and avoid injury in competition. Your boxing gloves and foot protectors also protect your opponent from punches and kicks. Without safety equipment, even a light blow can be very dangerous.

head guard

mouth guard

boxing gloves

groin protector

shin guards

foot protectors

WARMING UP

Before you start practising, you have to warm up your body to prevent injury.

Start with a rope, skipping for 10 minutes. Follow this with another 10 minutes of easy stretching. Repeat each of the exercises pictured 3 times for 15 seconds each. Don't stretch too far, in case you pull a muscle. You should feel just a slight strain each time you stretch.

Kick-boxing basics

You should repeat each basic technique of kick-boxing several times before progressing on to the next one.

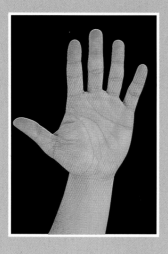  

You should always make a proper fist to avoid injury. Open both your hands flat, with your fingers apart. Fold back your fingers into your palm, and make a tight fist. Bind your fingers tightly with your thumb.

FIGHTING STANCE
Your posture should not be too tense or cramped. With this basic combat position, you can carry out every foot and fist technique. With both feet pointing forwards, the heel of your back foot should be lifted up slightly so that you can react quickly. Your knees should be bent, and your lower body turned slightly, to offer a very small target area. Your elbows should be close to your body. Lean your upper body slightly forward, chin close to your chest. Your head is protected by your shoulders and fists.

Jab

The jab is the most basic (and important) punch in kick-boxing. As well as being the quickest way to make contact with your opponent's head, it also helps you to judge the right distance from which to fight.

A jab can be made to the upper or lower part of your opponent's head.

The boxer on the right has dropped her protection and suffers a knockout.

1

2

3

THE BASIC JAB

1 Stand in the combat position and focus on your opponent.

2 Your rear hand should protect your face. Turn your hip and your shoulder into the punch. Put your weight on to your forward leg. At the moment you make contact with your opponent, turn your fist.

3 Immediately after the punch, pull your hitting arm back in a straight line for protection.

Right cross

If a fighter is on the floor for 10 seconds, that's a knockout, and the end of the bout. The right cross causes more knockouts than any other tactic.

1 Stand in the combat position and focus on your opponent, stepping forward on to your left foot.

2 Extend your arm from your shoulder to your opponent's head. Turn your fist into the opponent's face or body.

3 Shift your weight back on to your right foot, and use your left arm to protect your body and face.

1

2

3

Both boxers have dropped their protection, making them vulnerable to cross punches.

The boxer on the right skilfully keeps up his protection as he aims a right cross.

THAI PAD TECHNIQUE

Practising with a hand-held training pad (thai pad) helps you to improve your punching power. As your partner moves around with the pad, try to find the right distance from which to strike. Start slowly, then try some quicker moves. If you feel confident, try a right cross.

Uppercut

The uppercut is dangerous because the opponent's fist targets a small space between your defending hand and your chin.

A successful uppercut should gain power from the thrust of your legs and back, as well as your arm.

Stand in the combat position and focus on your opponent, with your weight on your forward leg and your knees slightly bent.

Straighten your legs to create an upward flow of power through your knees, hips and shoulders as you throw the punch.

Hook

The hook can be used in defence or attack. It should be landed with the elbow away from the body. As your hips and shoulders turn with the punch, the impact will be very great.

1

2

3

1 Stand in the combat position.
2 Turn your forward leg and arm in a quarter circle.

3 Raise your heel from the floor, and turn your whole left side into the punch. Use your rear arm to protect your face and body.

A hook should be from medium or close range.

Although it is difficult to master, the hook is a very dangerous knockout technique.

Front kick

The front kick is a fast manoeuvre that can be used to stop an opponent, or it can be a means of mid- or long-range attack. You should aim to make contact with the ball of your foot, striking your opponent's face or stomach. Your toes should not be straight, in case you injure them.

Stand in the combat position and focus on your opponent. As always, your feet should be roughly in line with your shoulders, with your body turned to the right. You should be leaning slightly forwards.

Raise your rear knee to the front. Pivot your standing leg to the side, while raising your knee. Turn your shoulder and rear arm forward.

Try to thrust your hip forwards, behind the kick. This will give the kick even more power, and enable you to kick over a long distance.

Snap your leg forward, pull your toes back and flex your foot. Follow the kick through with your hip. Try not to stretch your knee completely, because you can injure yourself with the power of the kick. It's important to snap your leg back again before setting your foot down.

With practice, you can aim a front kick at your opponent's head. Try to keep your balance at all times.

Roundhouse kick

The roundhouse kick is a powerful semicircular kick, which can be used at different heights. You hit your opponent with the top of your foot or with your shin.

To execute a successful roundhouse kick, try to use your shin to make contact with your opponent's body or head.

Stand in the combat position and focus on your opponent. Your left fist should be at about eye level, your right at cheek level.

Shift your weight on to your rear leg and turn the foot of the rear leg back. Turn on the ball of your foot. Raise your forward knee and keep your arms up.

To block a powerful roundhouse kick, you need to use two hands. If you are attempting a roundhouse, turn your hip completely into the kick to generate more power.

Kick in a semicircle, turning with your hip. Make sure you hold your arms tightly into your body.

After the kick, pull your foot down as quickly as possible, returning to the combat position to protect your body.

Side kick

Stand in the combat position and focus on your opponent.

The side kick is a very fast and powerful blow to the head or body. You should make contact with the heel or the side of your foot. The side kick gains much of its power from a twist of the hips which drives your foot forward into your opponent.

The boxer on the right tries to unbalance his opponent, who is attempting a side kick.

KICKING PRACTICE

Hold your partner's hand, and perform a side kick slowly 20 times without taking your foot down. This sort of practice not only sharpens your kicking technique, it also improves your balance, co-ordination and reactions.

Push your knee up quickly and turn your rear leg, with your heel pointing forwards.

Kick in a straight line. The side of your foot or your heel should hit your opponent's body. Turn your hip in the same direction.

Low kick

The low kick is a circular action that should land on your opponent's thigh, or preferably the shin. It often results in a knockout.

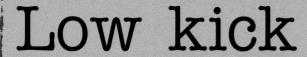

This well-executed and powerful low kick twists the opponent's leg to one side, pushing him off balance.

Step forward slightly and put your weight on to your front leg. Turn your hip, leg and rear arm forward.

Pivot your rear foot backwards. Turn your thigh, hip, side of your body and your swinging arm forward in a line. Push your swinging arm in a straight line towards your opponent's head. Use your second arm for protection, holding up your hands as you kick.

The low kick should be made from the same distance as a punching technique.

It is important to use your hip as the thrust for the whole movement of a low kick.

BLOCK AND COUNTER

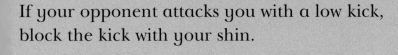

If your opponent attacks you with a low kick, block the kick with your shin.

If your opponent moves his or her foot down, that's the right time to counter with a front kick to the body.

Knee strike

The knee strike is a devastating technique, and it can enable a small boxer to overcome a larger, stronger opponent.

Muay Thai is a traditional form of kick-boxing, practised in Thailand. Knee strikes, kicks and throws win more points than punches.

The knee strike is a technique that is only allowed in Thai boxing, the toughest form of kick-boxing. In this discipline, you are allowed to use your knees and elbows to strike an opponent, and you can also throw them.

Adopt the fighting position.

Grab your opponent's head.

Pull his or her head down, push up your knee and push your hip forward.

Return to the fighting position.

PAD PRACTICE

If you want to practise the knee attack with all your power, your trainer must use thai pads. A good trainer will be able to withstand blows from both your knees in turn, as well as punches, kicks and elbow strikes. He or she can also vary the speed of your attack with movements of the pads.

Back kick

The back kick is one of the most powerful kicks in any martial art. It's often used to knock an opponent out. It should be delivered in one swift movement, making contact with the heel.

1

Make sure your partner is absolutely ready before practising a back kick.

Aim the back kick beneath the protection of your opponent's arms.

2

3

1 Stand in a combat position and focus on your opponent.
2 Raise the heel of your forward leg while turning your head back, keeping your eyes on your target. Pivot your hip and both legs at the same time.
3 Kick your leg straight back. It's important to turn as quickly as possible.

This is an example of perfect back kicking – striking the opponent beneath his arms, and into his body. The boxer who is kicking uses the swinging motion of his arms to generate more power. The kick should be executed in one super-quick movement.

Countering – punches

When your opponent throws a punch, it's not enough just to defend yourself – you should also launch a counter attack at the same time.

You can counter a jab with a straight front kick. Before the jab hits you, shift your weight back and kick with the forward leg at your opponent's body.

COUNTERING A JAB

1 Stand in the combat position.

2 Your opponent attacks you with a jab. With a side step, move out of the way, shifting your weight on to your rear leg.

3 As you start your counter, shift your weight back on to the front leg. At the same time, throw a punch at your opponent's head.

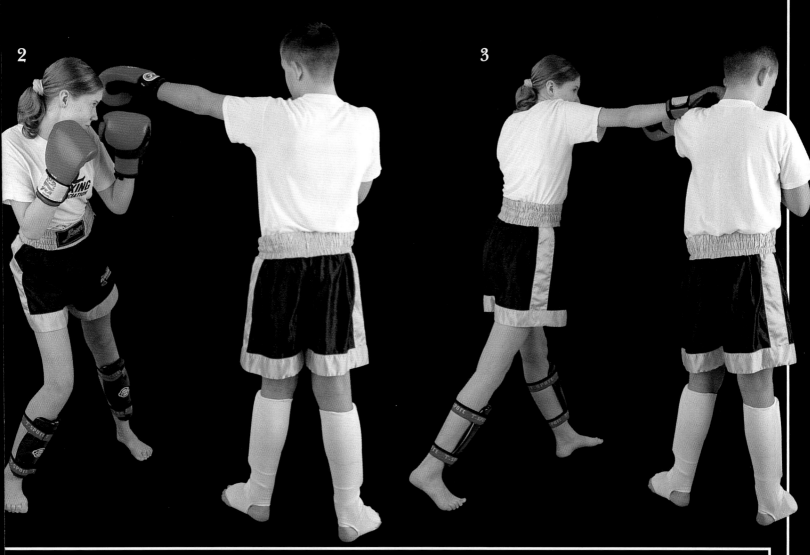

2

3

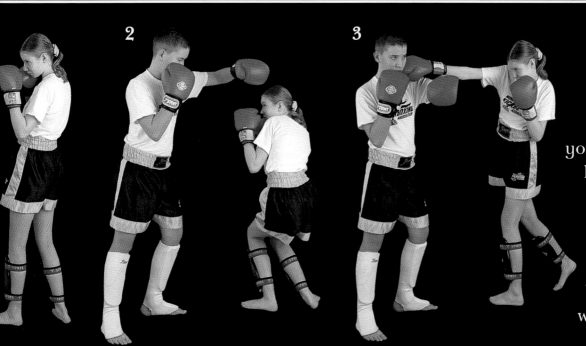

2

3

COUNTERING A HOOK

1 Stand in the combat position.
2 At the moment your opponent tries to hit you with a hook, duck down so that he misses.
3 With your opponent still off-balance, attack him with a powerful right cross to the head.

Countering – kicks

A kick is a powerful weapon – but it's worth remembering that if you are on the receiving end, your opponent will be slightly off-balance, and you can take advantage of this.

COUNTERING A SIDE KICK

1 Stand in the combat position.

2 As your opponent tries to hit you with a sidekick, take a step backwards so that he misses.

3 When your opponent starts to lower his foot, this is the time to make a counter move. Step forward and throw a long right cross at your opponent's chin.

COUNTERING A FRONT KICK.

1 Stand in the combat position.
2 As your opponent tries to hit you with a front kick, step to your right.

At the same time, turn your left arm down, scooping the front kick with your left forearm or boxing glove.

2

3

COUNTERING A ROUNDHOUSE KICK.

The roundhouse kick is a powerful technique, but it can be effectively countered. As your opponent tries to kick you with a roundhouse to the body, step to the left and counter directly with a low kick to the leg he is standing on. This should unbalance him and give you the advantage.

3

3 Counter with a low kick to your opponent's forward leg.

Useful information

Kick-boxing websites give advice on how to get started, training, techniques and competitions.

WORLD ASSOCIATION OF KICK-BOXING ORGANIZATIONS (WAKO)

www.wako-fikeda.it

INTERNATIONAL SPORT KICK-BOXING ASSOCIATION (ISKA)

www.iska.com

WORLD KICK-BOXING AND KARATE ASSOCIATION (WKA)

www.wka.co.uk

Useful addresses:
WAKO
Via Francesco Algarotti 4,
20124 Milan,
Italy
Tel: 00 39 2 67 077 030

ISKA
PO Box 90147,
Gainesville,
Florida,
32607-0147,
USA
Tel: 00 1 352 374 6876

WKA
James Court,
63 Gravely Lane,
Erdington,
B23 6LX,
UK
Tel: 00 44 121 382 2995

Kick-boxing terms

back kick powerful kick executed with a backward motion in a straight line

blocking stopping an opponent's blows with the arms, knees or hands

combat position stance adopted when ready to start boxing, your head protected by the shoulders and fists

dojo training studio

front kick straight forward kick executed with the ball of the kicking foot

hook sideways punch executed in a semicircular movement, elbow away from the body

jab short, sharp punch executed with the leading hand forward, arm extended from the body

knee strike blow from the knee to the opponent's body

knockout when a boxer cannot get up within 10 seconds

low kick derived from Thai Boxing, a kick from your shin to your opponent's thigh

right cross powerful punch executed with the rear hand

roundhouse kick semicircular kick

shadow boxing sparring practice with an imaginary opponent

side kick powerful kick executed sideways that hits its target in a straight line

sparring boxing practice between two kick-boxers

Thai boxing toughest form of kick-boxing which allows elbow strikes and throws that are prohibited in semi-, light- and full-contact kick-boxing

thai pad protective pads tied on to a trainer's forearms to enable the student to practise punches and kicks

uppercut powerful punch to the upper region of the body or head

WKA World Kick-boxing and Karate Association, the world's largest and oldest kick-boxing body

Index